Rhymes of a Storyteller
by Dave Southworth

Front and back cover design by Chip Southworth

Rhymes of a Storyteller
Author: Southworth, Dave

Copyright 2010 by Dave Southworth

ISBN: 978-1-890778-12-5
         1-890778-12-5

This book is a mixture of nonfiction and fiction.

All rights reserved. Without limiting the rights under copyright reserved above, no part of this book may be reproduced, stored in or introduced into a retrieval system, or transmitted, in any form or by any means (electronic, mechanical, photocopying, recording or otherwise) without the written permission of the copyright owner.

Contents

Preface	Page	7
Frozen Female	Page	9
The Demise of Rooster Red	Page	10
A Quest for Gold	Page	13
Sue's Mouse	Page	16
Candy Corn	Page	18
No Readin', Writin', or 'Rithmetic	Page	19
The Cigar Store Injun	Page	22
The Church Whistle	Page	24
The Legend of Silverheels	Page	25
The Acme Queen Parlor Organ	Page	27
Chihuahua	Page	29
The Ironclads	Page	30
Lost Brother, Lost Gold	Page	32
The Rumble Seat	Page	36
Pioneers	Page	38
Bullfrog	Page	40
The Punt Return	Page	41
"Boys, A Woman Has Your Flag"	Page	43
Colorado's Only Submarine	Page	44
Of Frail Mind	Page	46
The St. Augustine Lighthouse	Page	47
The Vanishing Duelists	Page	49
Antelope Canyon	Page	50
Oh, Those Birds	Page	51
Big Hat	Page	52
Broken Nose Scotty	Page	53
A Frontier Kitchen	Page	55
Judge Roy Bean	Page	57
Contemplating	Page	59
Creede	Page	60
A Ghost Town	Page	62
The Salute	Page	64
Pirogue on the Bayou	Page	65
Simple Sam	Page	66
Gay Rights and Wrongs	Page	68
Pegleg Bodeen	Page	69
Whiskey Lake	Page	71
How Politicians Duck Questions	Page	72
My '55 T-Bird	Page	73
Cockeyed Gail	Page	74
The Portland Head Light	Page	76
Fat Rat and Heartless Matt	Page	78
Biltmore House	Page	80
Pig Wrestling	Page	83
Sarcastic Camper	Page	85
Places with Goofy Names	Page	86

PREFACE

Most of the rhymes, or poems, in this book are nonfiction. They are stories of people and places that have been set to various patterns of verse and rhyme. The author doesn't claim to be a poet, only a storyteller who enjoys using different rhyme schemes to convey his short stories, without too much concern for ideal or faultless meter. Ten different rhyme arrangements are used in the composition of these stories, which are: abab cdcd; abcb defe; abb cdd; abcbdb efgfhf; aa bb cc; aaba aaca; abbb cddd ee; aabb ccdd; aaaa bbbb; and aaaaaa bbbbbb. Some have slight variations. Use of consonance is rare. Blank or free verse is only used when an actual quotation is included.

With exception, most of the rhyming sounds herewith are one or two syllables regardless of whether the words contain one, two or more syllables. One syllable rhyming sounds are found in one-syllable words and in words in which the primary or secondary stress falls on the final syllable, as in *orthodox* and *fox*. Also, many words in the English language have more than one standard pronunciation. Occasionally, certain words may not rhyme for every reader. Enjoy this little book for the stories it contains and for the fun of the rhymes, without being too critical of form.

"Frozen Female" is obviously fiction. The yarn was actually conceived by Orth Stein, a writer for the *Chronicle* in Leadville, Colorado. This author has set Stein's story to verse. A tale that grew out of the mining camps of Colorado is the "Legend of Silverheels." Nothing exists to substantiate the story, although many people believe that it actually happened. "Lost Brother, Lost Gold," and "Big Hat" may simply be a part of mining camp lore. "The Demise of Rooster Red," "Simple Sam," "Cockeyed Gail," "A Quest for Gold," "The Cigar Store Injun," "Pig Wrestling," "Fat Rat and Heartless Matt," "Pegleg Bodeen," "Sarcastic Camper," "Candy Corn," and "The Punt Return" are strictly figments of the author's imagination. "How Politicians Duck Questions," "Gay Rights and Wrongs," and "Contemplating" are opinions. You may agree or disagree.

Most of the other stories are true, or believed by most to be factual. Yes, even "Sue's Mouse" is a true story that occurred in Littleton, Colorado in 1996. This author has taken the liberty of twisting Clement Clarke Moore's poem, "Twas the Night before Christmas" (that was penned in 1822) to suit the occasion of the mouse in Sue's house.

Rhymes of a Storyteller is light, entertaining reading that is suitable for all ages.

FROZEN FEMALE

This story was told by a fellow named Stein.
I wasn't born yet, so it couldn't be mine.

He was a journalist, who was ahead of his time.
I have simply taken his tale and set it to rhyme.

So, if you don't believe a word that you see,
blame it on Stein, don't blame it on me.

Stein worked for the *Chronicle* up in Leadville,
where many a yarn was penned by his quill.

His imaginative tales one would not want to miss.
One such fantasy went something like this.

Amidst wintery ice and snow all around,
a female prospector's frozen body was found.

She was overcome by nature as she panned a creek,
below the headwaters of Homestake Peak.

It would be foolish to take the stiff to a graveyard,
for a hole couldn't be dug as the ground was too hard.

So, she was strapped to a burro upside down,
and taken to the *Chronicle* office in the middle of town.

Her body was placed on a desk by the pot-bellied stove.
What happened next was a shocker, by Jove.

The newsmen watched as she thawed out, limb by limb.
Suddenly, she sat up and gave a big grin.

Then she stood and walked out the office door,
never to be heard from evermore.

THE DEMISE OF ROOSTER RED

This is the story of a large, decrepit barn,
      located somewhere in rural Lee County.
And, a fighting gamecock named Rooster Red,
      upon whom there was a very large bounty.

On the second Sunday of every month,
      people would flock to the barn from afar,
To barter and bet on their favorites,
      and to watch the fierce cocks spar.

Gamecock fights are against the law,
      but the old barn was on the sheriff's farm.
So, people could bring their fighters and money,
      knowing they would be safe from harm.

The old, creaking barn was the venue,
      and in the center was the sparring ring.
The game was elimination, with the cocks fighting
      'til one was left standing, to be dubbed "King."

There were many fighters each second Sunday,
      But, one cock stood out above all the rest.
He had been King for several months,
      and was considered the very best.

No gamecock could defeat this invincible one,
      whose name was Rooster Red.
So, the show's promoters decided that they
      should put a bounty on his head.

A thousand dollars would be awarded to
      any owner whose gamecock could beat
the unconquerable Rooster Red,
      who had never tasted defeat.

Folks that were there will never forget
    the day of Sunday the twenty-first.
There was a violent storm, but the show went on,
    with the weather at its worst.

As usual, Rooster Red kept winning,
    but so did another cock with no name.
They clawed their way past every foe,
    'til they were the only two left in the game.

Rooster Red was an overwhelming favorite
    to maintain his title as King.
Betting was heavy and the money flowed,
    as the birds were tossed into the ring.

At that instant, lightning struck the old barn,
    and a plank tore loose from above.
The lights went out and the barn was pitch black.
    and frightened people began to shove.

But, as quickly as that, the lights came back on,
    and to the ring turned every head.
Beneath the plank from the roof lay the invincible one.
    Rooster Red was dead.

The cock with no name strutted about,
    and his owner was mighty proud.
Those who bet on Rooster Red lost their money.
    "Foul" was the cry from the crowd.

The cock with no name was declared the winner,
    amidst all of the crowd's demanding.
Rules are rules, however,
    and he was the last gamecock standing.

The lucky cock was declared new "King,"
    and furthermore claimed the bounty,
But, Sunday the twenty-first at the sheriff's barn,
    was the last cockfight ever in Lee County.

A QUEST FOR GOLD

Ten feet of snow,
        and the mountain air cold.
Too cold you would think
        to be panning for gold.

One man stubbornly chose to
        endure the pain.
He must have had ice-water
        running in each vein.

Like all prospectors
        he had a dream,
That he'd discover gold
        while panning a stream.

On and on he trudged,
        through snow and rain.
Would you consider him stalwart,
        or think him insane?

Well, regardless of what you might
        think of the man,
Let me tell you, he finally found
        traces of gold in his pan.

The tiny gold flakes
        gave him great hope.
He envisioned a mother lode
        further up the slope.

He calculated and calculated
        as to where to dig.
Then found his spot,
        and set up his jig.

T'was it, he was sure,
        and staked his claim.
Then registered the property
        with a proper name.

He dug an opening
        deep and wide.
Then tunneled into
        the mountainside.

The thirst for gold
        was what made him tick.
He worked himself sick
        with shovel and pick.

By kerosene light
        he worked day and night,
And expedited the process
        with dynamite.

Where, he wondered, was
        that golden vein,
That was supposed to bring him
        riches and fame.

With nothing to show
        for all of his pain,
Was this tunnel really
        a worthless claim?

He became more disgruntled
        as time went on.
His supplies and gold dust
        were nearly gone.

A wasted life, he thought,
    and made his call,
By deciding that it was time
    to end it all.

Only one stick of dynamite
    left to use,
So he held it tightly,
    and lit the fuse.

Time passed, and folks wondered
    as to his whereabout.
So, they climbed up to his claim
    to check things out.

The prospector's remains lay
    stiff and cold,
Beside a dazzling vein of
    very pure gold.

SUE'S MOUSE

Twas the night before Labor Day, and all through Sue's house
Not a creature was stirring, except maybe a mouse.
Sue's wet stockings were hung, on the shower rod with care,
In hopes they'd be dry, so tomorrow she could wear.

Sue's cat was nestled all snug in his bed,
While visions of tasty mice danced in his head.
Sue had put on her nightie, and had her nightcap,
And had just settled in for a much needed nap.

When behind the stove there arose such a clatter,
Sue's cat sprang from his bed to see what was the matter.
Away to the kitchen he flew like a flash,
With Sue right behind in a sprinter's dash.

The oven light reflecting on the white floor tile,
Gave the luster of mid-day to the domicile.
When what to their wondering eyes should appear,
But a miniature mouse, around the stove did peer.

With a little jump, so lively and quick,
The mouse disappeared as quick as a wink.
"Oh," thought the cat, "t'would be better then grouse,"
What a nice meal I could make of that mouse."

"Oh," thought Sue, "What a cute little mouse,"
"A nice addition to have around the house."
The little mouse she was determined to please,
So every night on a dish she would place some cheese.

Now cheese, Sue's cat would always shun,
But, every single morning the dish would have none.
When she spied that empty dish, for joy she would jump,
'Cause she knew her mouse was getting plump.

She discovered she had no cheese, one stormy night,
A predicament she set out to promptly right.
With her umbrella she headed to the grocery store,
In the midst of a sloppy, nasty downpour.

When the store clerk saw Sue, his little round belly,
Shook as he laughed, like a bowl full of jelly.
Though drenched, she purchased some cheese for her mouse,
Then swiftly splashed her way back to her house.

She put some cheese in the dish, even though it was late,
Certain that her mouse would appreciate.
Then she put on her nightie, and had her nightcap,
And settled in for a much needed nap.

She sprang from her bed, to the alarm clock's whistle,
To the kitchen she flew, like the down of a thistle.
On the floor lay her cat looking quite hale,
Hanging from his mouth was the mouse's tail.

CANDY CORN

I've had a craving for candy corn.
Almost since the day I was born.
About the time that diapers were worn.
Could be 'cause I'm a Capricorn.

You ask, which part do I like best.
That is such a silly request.
I can advise, 'cause I've put it to the test.
The top part is better than all the rest.

You ask, which segment is the top part.
Such a foolish query from one so smart.
It depends upon which end you start.
The top is opposite from the bottom part.

You ask which part is on the bottom.
Another question that's kind of dumb.
It goes without saying, by rule of thumb,
if the tip points up, yellow's the bottom.

White is the bottom if the tip points down,
and if that be the case the yellow's the crown.
But if you get mixed up and turn it around,
the candy corn might be upside down.

You ask, which part do I like best.
That is such a silly request.
I can advise, 'cause I've put it to the test.
The top part is better than all the rest.

NO READIN', WRITIN', OR 'RITHMETIC

John D. Morrissey was a miner,
    known for his fortune and fame.
His wealth came from his mining claim,
    his fame 'cause his brain was a little lame.

Not only could he not read or write,
    but his knowledge of arithmetic was slight.

Morrissey wasn't totally dumb,
    he simply lacked an education.
His calculation and computation
    often brought about consternation.

Morrissey once hollered into one of his shafts,
    "How many down there are ye?"
He then responded to an answer of, "Three,"
    "Half of you come up and have a drink with me."

Not only could he not read or write,
    but his knowledge of arithmetic was slight.

Morrissey carried a fancy gold pocket watch,
    with a fob and diamond inlay.
He didn't know how to tell the time of day,
    but the watch he loved to display.

He would pull out his watch without delay,
    when asked if he had the time of day,
"See for yourself," Morrissey would say,
    "Then you'll know I'm not lying in any way."

Not only could he not read or write,
    but his knowledge of arithmetic was slight.

He would pull out his watch and hand it to another,
    if he wanted to know the time himself.
"On the correct time," he would say, "I've bet myself,"
    "If I'm right, a smoke and drink I'll buy thyself."

Then he would say, "I bet myself that its 4 o'clock,"
    but of his guess he was never sure.
So his bet was always safe and secure,
    and the correct time he would always procure.

Not only could he not read or write,
    but his knowledge of arithmetic was slight.

John Morrissey couldn't sign his name,
    so he always had excuses for doing same.
"My fist is swollen and I can't hold a pen," he would claim,
    one of many reasons that he could blame.

He once showed up at a hotel front desk,
    with his palm wrapped up in a band.
"Sign my name for me," was his demand,
    "I just slammed the buggy door on my hand."

Not only could he not read or write,
    but his knowledge of arithmetic was slight.

When a local church needed a chandelier,
    for its cost he agreed to spring.
But he added, in shades of a ding-a-ling,
    "I'll be darned if I know who will play on the thing."

The decision was made to purchase some gondolas,
    for a resort hotel being developed nearby.
When Morrissey was asked how many they should buy,
    "Just get two, and let them breed," was his reply.

Not only could he not read or write,
   but his knowledge of arithmetic was slight.

THE CIGAR STORE INJUN

Gramps was known to have a nip and a chew,
and stogies, I'll tell ya, t'was more than a few.
Fact is, that about every two weeks, or so,
he'd be buyin' a new supply of gin and tobacco.

Granny could tolerate a cigar and a chaw,
but when it came to his nippin', a line she would draw.
So, he'd hide his booze on a shelf high in the outhouse,
where no one would find it, especially his spouse.

I often wondered if Granny knew why he'd camp,
out in the privy, for hours with his lamp.
When the outhouse ran dry, it'd be time fer buyin',
to resupply his shelf with a new stock of gin.

Gramps would hitch the old hoss up to the buckboard,
and Granny'd make a list of things they could afford.
Because Gramps had no idea of how to read,
she would draw pictures of what we would need.

If I hadn't been bad, he'd let me go too,
and there wasn't nuthin' that I'd rather do.
He'd let me ride up top 'n hold the reins,
to guide the old hoss across the plains.

My main reason for going was to visit the wooden Injun,
standing in front of the store where Gramps bought his gin.
He was a lonely statue that couldn't speak a word,
but, when I spoke to him, I was sure that he heard.

His body of red was covered in war paint,
and his feet were bare, but he had no complaint.
On his headdress was carved many a feather,
and his skin was tough, to withstand the weather.

His face was marred with lots of scars,
and in his hand he held a batch of cigars.
It seemed like he was giving a gift, not going to war,
but, I imagin' he was also advertising the store.

The Injun always had time to listen, so I just kept talking',
'cause it always took Gramps forever to do his shoppin'.
The wooden Injun needed a name, t'was my belief,
But I didn't know the name of nary a chief.

Then I remembered a chief that Granny had talked about,
And decided that name would be fittin' no doubt.
I was glad to see Gramps in the outhouse, sippin' his gin,
'cause it was that much sooner that I could see the Injun,

named CHIEF JUSTICE!

THE CHURCH WHISTLE

Worship, at the camp of Red Mountain,
was in a state of poor condition.
Not only was there not a preacher,
but there wasn't nary a mission.

So, the Reverend William Davis
to that mining camp was sent.
He received a very cool reception,
however, much to his lament.

The saloons wouldn't let him preach
and neither would the dance hall.
His only audience out on the street,
was two burros, and that was all.

Well, the Reverend packed his bags,
and moved over to Guston nearby.
So cordial was his welcome there,
its sinners he began to sanctify.

The folks there wanted a church,
so they lent a helping hand.
Money was donated from near and far,
as were the pews and the land.

The little church became a reality,
with the Reverend Davis as its preacher.
Up in the chapel's belfry, however,
was a most unusual feature.

It is the only church known anywhere,
that prior to a reading of an Epistle,
it announced its services far and wide,
with the shrill blast from a mine whistle.

THE LEGEND OF SILVERHEELS

Buckskin Joe was the mining camps name.
So dubbed for the fellow who filed the first claim.
T'was a rowdy camp, with much ado,
And the place where the legend of Silverheels grew.

No one seems to know her real name,
Or furthermore from whence she came.
Silverheels was a charming dance hall girl,
With heels of silver, and a choker of pearl.

Her heels would glitter whenever she twirled,
And, her calves would show whenever she whirled.
She was the girl the men seemed to prefer,
And, they clamored for a chance to dance with her.

Tragedy befell the camp in the winter of '61.
By an epidemic of smallpox, the community was overrun.
Mines, stores and saloons shut down,
Desperately ill were most miners in town.

Silverheels' boyfriend died, as the sickness spread,
There was a steady trek to the graveyard to bury the dead.
As the highly contagious disease got worse,
Word went out from the camp for help from a nurse,

The call for help went unheeded, however,
For those that survived were left pockmarked forever.
And, no woman was willing to risk life or beauty,
No matter how urgent the call was for duty.

Throughout the ordeal, Silverheels helped the ailing,
Caring for the sick and comforting the dying.
From cabin to cabin, and hour by hour,
She would scrub, nurse, cook and scour.

Finally, she too was stricken by the affliction.
She locked her door in self-imposed restriction.
Eventually the epidemic did subside,
And, activity in the camp was back in stride.

To show their gratitude for her helping hand,
The men collected a reward that totaled five grand.
T'was a fitting tribute for the girl they endeared.
They took it to her cabin, to find that she had disappeared.

For all of her friends, she had sacrificed her beauty,
Then shunned her admirers, as well as the booty.
Later, in the cemetery was seen a female with bowed head.
When approached, the veiled woman quickly fled.

It must have been Silverheels, mourning her boyfriend,
At least that is what the miners contend.
In appreciation of the brave girl's valor,
A majestic peak, Mt. Silverheels, was named in her honor.

To look up at the summit at the silvery snow,
Reminds one of the heroine of Buckskin Joe.

THE ACME QUEEN PARLOR ORGAN

Available from the Sears, Roebuck
    catalogue of 1902,
is the Acme Queen Parlor Organ,
    direct from factory to you.

Its tone is so pure
    that its sure to please,
as fingers dance
    upon its keys.

There is no equal
    to their instruments,
or the price of
    27 dollars, and 45 cents.

To reach you in perfect condition,
    is guaranteed,
and a 5 dollar freight charge
    it shouldn't exceed.

The organ is 3 1/2 feet wide,
    and 6 feet tall,
and weighs 350 pounds
    boxed for the haul.

Carved from solid oak
    is its beautiful case.
Nickel plated pedal frames
    adorn the organs base.

Sears, Roebuck & Company's
    policy is firm.
Cash in advance with the order,
    is their only term.

Included is an instructional book,
    a very valuable tool,
and with every Acme Queen,
    you receive a free organ stool.

CHIHUAHUA

Chihuahua was a short-lived mining town,
    high in the mountains where the air is thin.
There was no doctor's office or chapel,
    Nor a doctor or preacher within.
The residents boasted that none were needed,
    because there wasn't any sickness or sin.

Then one day, two prospectors were robbed and killed,
    in the town's first tragedy.
A posse set out in pursuit of the scoundrels,
    as they attempted to flee.
Three of the rogues were tracked down and caught,
    then hanged from the nearest tree.

The posse achieved revenge for the dastardly deed,
    as the killers' escape they were able to foil.
Now three for two is fair exchange,
    but to dig five graves in the hard mountain soil,
Would be too much to ask
    for any gravedigger to toil.

Somewhere near the townsite of Chihuahua,
    there are two separate gravesites.
So the good guys and bad guys don't have to share a plot,
    on those cold and lonely nights.
The preacher who wasn't needed in that "sinless" town,
    wasn't there to give last rites.

THE IRONCLADS

The Civil War naval battle
    between the Monitor and Merrimac,
put the art of shipbuilding
    on a totally new track.

The battle proved the effectiveness
    of ironclad ships,
and established a pattern for
    future battleships.

The Merrimac that was originally
    constructed of oak,
was sunk by the Federals when
    they abandoned Norfolk.

Confederates raised the vessel
    and put her into repair,
then they diligently readied her
    for warfare.

To her hull they proceeded
    to laminate
a very heavy gauge of
    iron plate.

They topped her off with
    more of the same,
then added ten heavy guns to
    the crown of her frame.

Considerably smaller was the
    ironclad Monitor,
but, her ability to maneuver made her
    a fine warrior.

The Monitor was also combat-ready
    and prepared for war,
with a two-gun turret above
    her coat of armor.

On the 9th of March
    in the year of '62,
the vessels squared off
    out on the blue.

The harbor at Hampton Roads
    was the battle scene,
for the first conflict between armored ships
    that the world had ever seen.

For three long hours they
    bombarded one another,
with neither being able to sink
    the other.

No sailor was killed, and few required
    a bandage,
as the Monitor was unscathed, and the Merrimac
    had little damage.

This historic battle
    set the stage, however,
for navies of the world
    to build ironclads forever.

LOST BROTHER, LOST GOLD

The thought of striking it rich
    fueled a million dreams.
And, many dreamers headed west,
    in order to pan its streams.

One was George Skinner, who ventured to
    the Sangre de Cristo range.
Brother Bill declined to go with him,
    and his mind, George couldn't change.

Several months after George departed,
    Bill received a letter in the mail.
Should he decide to follow, George advised,
    as to how to pick up his trail.

Months passed, then a year or two,
    and a second letter never came.
So, Bill headed west to find George,
    in that mountainous terrain.

He inquired of every prospector he saw,
    as to his brother's whereabouts.
Nobody knew anything, and weeks went by,
    all of which raised his doubts.

Finally, an old man gave him a lead,
    "I think I might know of whom you speak.
There was a fellow named Skinner
    that was prospecting up on Horn's Peak."

The old-timer added that he hadn't seen
    Skinner for a year or two.
It was the first news that Bill had heard,
    and at least it gave him a clue.

He hired a guide, and they packed a burro
        with food and supplies for the mountain trail.
To Horn's Peak they went and searched everywhere,
        but their efforts were to no avail.

In an abandoned log cabin,
        they decided to take cover,
from an afternoon storm,
        until it blew over.

The burro stood outside with his neck through a window,
        in order to keep his head dry.
And, they all continued on with their search,
        as soon as they had a clear sky.

A short piece up the trail,
        the normally sure-footed burro
slipped on wet mud and tumbled
        into the gorge below.

With their supplies far beneath them,
        Bill and his guide
had no choice but to climb
        down the mountainside.

They reached their recently departed burro,
        and as they began to unpack,
they spied skeletons of a human and another burro
        to whose bones was strapped a sack.

They also must have slipped off the narrow
        trail at nearly the same spot.
Bill removed the sack from the bones,
        and cautiously untied its knot.

Inside he discovered
    two pouches together.
One was light, one was heavy,
    and both made of leather.

The heavy pouch contained, to their amazement,
    a fortune in nearly pure gold.
In the lighter pouch was a diary,
    with a cover scribed in bold.

As he read the inscription
    Bill's heart sank to his stomach.
"George Skinner's Diary," it said,
    and t'was worse'n a mule's kick.

His worst fears were realized,
    for there lay George,
beside his burro,
    at the bottom of the gorge.

Bill also discovered an unfinished letter
    that George had been writing to him,
telling of his rich strike, and how to find it
    should something happen to him.

The letter described the gulch that
    lay below his find,
but contained no specific details
    on how to find the mine.

Bill buried George's remains,
    And the two burros as well.
The chill of winter was setting in
    as the snow lightly fell.

So, as Bill and his guide
        retreated from Horn's Peak,
they agreed to return in the spring,
        and the rich mine they would seek.

Well, they did return
        that following spring,
and the next three springs, as well,
        but never found a thing.

They left believing that every inch of
        ground was covered.
Evidently the gold is still there,
        waiting to be rediscovered.

THE RUMBLE SEAT

Back in the 1940s,
    Grandpa owned the coolest car.
It was a Packard coupe with a rumble seat,
    the grooviest car on the road, by far.

I can't think of anything that was more fun,
    than riding with my brother in the rumble seat.
Bless her heart, our little sister had to ride up front,
    and couldn't enjoy the treat.

Grandpa's black Packard
    was a prestigious automobile,
and its style and grace
    had great appeal.

Up front was a fancy hood ornament,
    with its wings swept back.
Behind the rumble seat in the rear,
    was a classy looking luggage rack.

Wire wheels with a little red hex in the center,
    added to the fashionable ride,
and a spare tire was encased and mounted
    into the front fender on each side.

Those fenders flowed into running boards,
    upon which one could step.
It was on the rumble seat's two steps, however,
    that my brother and I were adept.

Seat belts hadn't yet been invented,
    so it was a thing we never thought about,
if Grandpa had hit a bump in the road,
    I guess we could have bounced out,

It was awesome to ride in Grandpa's rumble seat,
    up and down each hill.
Sometimes I wish we were kids again,
    so we could relive the thrill.

PIONEERS

Into each wagon was stuffed
    everything they could carry,
as pioneers heading west
    traversed the wide prairie.

Through rain storms and ill-health,
    hardship and pain,
dust storms and starvation,
    and the most difficult terrain.

Many had to circle their wagons,
    as they crossed the great plains,
when Indian warriors threatened
    encroaching wagon trains.

Following a journey filled with
    privation and tribulation,
most of the hardy pioneers
    eventually reached their destination.

Those who arrived as winter's cold
    a burden of snow would bring,
often had to live in their wagon,
    until the thaw of spring.

Life in those earliest cabins
    required much fortitude,
as most were thrown together with logs
    in a manner unquestionably crude.

Gaps in the roof were filled with dirt,
    that would turn to mud in the rain,
and on to the occupants below
    the mud would drip and drain.

Those who had been rolling in wagons,
    however, with canvas over their bed,
weren't inclined to be too fastidious
    about the roof over their head.

Once a sawmill was constructed,
    improvements to cabins were made,
Pioneer life became more comfortable,
    and the hardships began to fade.

BULLFROG

The bullfrog is a very large
    species of frogs
        that makes its home in stagnant bogs

Or, still ponds
    with lots of lily pads, it seems,
    but they never ever frequent streams.

They have four large feet
    and huge eyes by scale,
    but nary will you ever find a tail.

They can spring three yards
    in a single leap,
    and jump a bank that's fairly steep.

One can even bound that far
    with another clinging to its back,
    like a bronco buster riding bareback.

For a short distance they can
    equal the speed of a horse,
    racing on its swiftest course.

They have a monstrous roaring croak,
    much like the sound of a bull,
    more hoarse, yet powerful.

When there are many bullfrogs together,
    they make such a horrid noise,
    that to the human ear, it obviously annoys.

If you have thoughts of moving to Pennsylvania,
    don't buy a house on a pond or a bog,
    or you'll forever be disturbed by the nervy bullfrog.

THE PUNT RETURN

A miracle is what we need
if victory we are to claim.
We are down five points
with ten seconds left in the game.

It's fourth down and they must punt,
it might be the very last play.
Our only hope is to block that kick,
or run it back all of the way.

The clock will start,
with the snap of the ball.
It's as tense a moment
as we can recall.

There are ten fast men up on the line
hoping to block the punt,
with our isolated return man behind
without any blockers in front.

Oh, they got the kick away
and our guy backpedals to make the catch
as a herd of eleven men converge
in a very perilous mismatch.

The punt return man darts up the middle
hoping to split the seam.
His legs churning and driving
as he picks up steam.

He shakes off one tackle,
then another, and another,
as he cuts to the sideline
and fakes out one other.

Past the visitor's bench he speeds,
and he finally breaks into the clear.
Thirty, twenty, ten, touchdown,
as our fans let out a deafening cheer.

There are zeros on the clock
as victory we claim,
and our great punt return man
is the hero of the game.

"BOYS, A WOMAN HAS YOUR FLAG"

South of Nashville, in March of 1863,
a battle occurred at Thompson's Station, Tennessee.
Near a place called Homestead Manor,
an incident happened of great courage and valor.

General Earl Van Dorn led the Confederate stand,
to stop a Federal thrust, and to protect their land.
Seventeen year-old Alice Thompson watched the war
from a Homestead Manor cellar door.

She saw the Confederate color-bearer shot with a Union round,
then stagger and fall, and his flag hit the ground.
Alice dashed from the basement without despair,
grabbed the flag and hoisted it high in the air.

Colonel Samuel Earle was amazed by her lack of fear.
"Boys, a woman has your flag," he bellowed, so all could hear.
Moved by her bravery, the men let out a "Rebel Yell,"
and the Yankee advances they were able to repel.

While holding the flag, a shell splattered her with dirt,
but it didn't explode, and Alice was unhurt.
Discretion, the Rebs thought, is the better part of valor,
and they escorted Alice safely back to the cellar.

The Confederates won the battle at Thompson's Station,
capturing 1,300 Yanks during the confrontation.
The victory was aided in part by a young woman's determination,
but roughly two years later Federal forces would unite the nation.

COLORADO'S ONLY SUBMARINE

Central City was an unlikely place
    for a ship designer to reside.
But this story is one we should retrace,
    though it didn't occur by the seaside.

R. T. Owens didn't want to move,
    and he had a new design,
that he hoped the Navy would approve,
    and to him a new contract assign.

He believed that he had a brainstorm
    for a more efficient submarine.
One that would outperform
    any the world had ever seen.

So he rented a livery stable
    in which to construct his ship.
Two carpenters who were very able,
    were hired for their workmanship.

The sub was eighteen feet long,
    and constructed of hand-hewn lumber.
It was stitched with square nails to make it strong,
    then covered with metal sheets of great number.

Missouri Lake froze, nearly fifty years later,
    at a level lower than usual.
Beneath the ice, to the awe of a skater,
    was sighted something very unusual.

So this thing they could further inspect,
    folks removed large chunks of ice.
The long, dark, cigar-shaped object
    was then raised with a hoisting device.

Sure enough, the strange looking mass,
   was the R. T. Owens boat.
The design would never have interested Navy brass,
   because the submarine wouldn't float.

OF FRAIL MIND

John Dugan was better known as Rain-in-the-Face,
    although nobody really knows why.
He was a harmless, simple-minded old soul.
    Simple-minded is where the emphasis should lie.

It is said, that he once spent years
    in an orchard back in Arkansas,
digging in futility for buried treasure,
    before he decided to withdraw.

His constitution reflected many years of
    tiresome labor and pain,
from prospecting Colorado hills with pick and shovel,
    but success he would never attain.

To the south he'd walk for days each fall,
    to spend winters where there wasn't much snow.
Then he'd head back to the mountains to search,
    for the pot at the end of the rainbow.

He spent two years driving a tunnel,
    supposedly to explore,
For a long lost hidden treasure
    vault of high yield ore.

T'was on another man's location, it is said,
    that Rain-in-the-Face staked his claim.
Had he found a bonanza, the riches wouldn't have been his,
    and he would have toiled in vain.

Frail minded Rain-in-the-Face just drifted along,
    as though he owned the earth.
To some, living in poverty and being content
    obviously has its worth.

THE ST. AUGUSTINE LIGHTHOUSE

Adjacent to St. Augustine,
    near the north end of a strand,
sits the historical lighthouse
    on Anastasia Island.

After founding the area
    in the year of 1565,
Pedro Menendez built a watchtower
    to help the new settlement survive.

The original structure, constructed of wood,
    was replaced in 1683,
by a guard tower built from coquina,
    enclosed by a wall close to the sea.

In 1824, ten large oil lamps
    were added to the tower's peak.
Florida's first lighthouse was created,
    at the time a structure unique.

Appointed was Juan Andreu
    as St. Augustine's first light keeper.
His cousin, Joseph Andreu,
    followed as his successor.

After Joseph fell to his death
    while painting the lighthouse,
the first female keeper was named,
    Maria, who was Joseph's spouse.

T'was the keeper's role to carry the oil,
    also the glass to cleanse,
and to continually remove the soot
    from the face of the Fresnel lens.

During the Civil War
> the Confederacy extinguished the light,
to help prevent a Union attack
> through the darkness of the night.

As the ocean encroached on
> the old coquina location,
a new brick lighthouse was built
> on a concrete foundation.

In 1874, its light first shone,
> with new lens of the first degree.
Six years later the old coquina tower
> collapsed right into the sea.

The top of the lighthouse is
> 165 feet above sea level.
There are 219 steps to
> the observation level.

St. Augustine's light finally
> received electrical power,
and keepers were no longer needed
> at the lighthouse tower.

For vessels entering the harbor,
> the light still shines as their escort,
to the nation's oldest city,
> and the nation's oldest port.

THE VANISHING DUELISTS

In the early days of Breckenridge,
    two miners were involved in a heated dispute.
So serious was the squabble,
    the other, each one threatened to shoot.

Judge Silverthorne contemplated the matter,
    then made a decision you might think cruel.
Realizing that someone would get shot anyway,
    he ruled that they should engage in a duel.

The two were to stand back to back,
    walk fifteen paces, then turn and fire.
As they each took those crucial steps,
    disaster loomed, desperate and dire.

The countdown continued, fourteen, fifteen,
    but instead of turning, both men ran,
In opposite directions,
    never to be seen again.

ANTELOPE CANYON

Arizona's awesome Antelope Canyon
is a sight to see that parallels none.
Sandstone carved by wind and rain,
a wondrous beauty, hard to explain.

For millenniums its wondrous scape
was forged by nature to take its shape.
Narrow passageways a few feet wide
have a sandy floor on which to stride.

Shafts of light from slots at the rim,
brighten rock colors as the beams skim.
Rust orange, yellow, gray and red,
from entrance to exit to overhead.

Though a picture they often say,
a thousand words be worth, it may.
No matter how good, it will not match,
the see for yourself image you will catch.

Sandstone carved by wind and rain,
a wondrous beauty, hard to explain.
It's a great site, so take a companion,
to see the incredible Antelope Canyon.

OH, THOSE BIRDS!

I'm glad to hear you are coming to see me.
Turn at the mailbox, my name you will see.

You can't miss it, if you arrive during daylight.
It's the only drive speckled black and white.

Don't bring a convertible with the top down.
A wide-brimmed hat will protect your crown.

No, we are not expecting any rain.
Hold on and I will further explain!

Trees cover every inch of the driveway.
Do you understand what I am trying to say?

There's a reason why everything's black and white.
Bird droppings create a considerable blight.

The birds here seem to be a little dumber.
They don't know how to go north in the summer.

I hope this situation does not displease,
because I love the birds and I love the trees.

BIG HAT

Redcliff was a typical mining town,
   with a brass band, several saloons and a cemetery.
The first man buried there
   was killed by a bear, so said his obituary.

Cloth partitions separated rooms
   at the primitive Star Hotel.
Sleeping conditions were pitiful,
   but their chow was considered swell.

Redcliff had a dance hall girl
   who was affectionately known as "Big Hat."
She wasn't skinny and she wasn't fat,
   she wasn't busty, but she wasn't flat.

On a stage or dance floor her
   rhythmic moves were lively and quick.
Men put up a fuss to dance with her,
   for she was the miners' first pick.

Big Hat became distressed and despondent,
   influenced by much alcohol.
One day the tearful dance hall girl
   decided to "end it all."

She ran to the bank of Turkey Creek,
   and threw herself in with a mighty leap.
Her effort was futile, however, for she
   jumped into water only four inches deep.

BROKEN NOSE SCOTTY

Scotty was a storyteller and a dreamer,
with an easy-going, pleasant, mannerly demeanor.
He gave up his life as a teamster, to search for silver and gold.
His rags to riches to rags scenario is a story to be told.

While driving a stagecoach near Weston Pass,
Scotty lost control when a wheel hit a crevice.
The runaway stage went downhill in a flash,
and then hit a boulder with a terrible crash.

For nearly a mile the luggage was scattered.
Scotty and others were bruised and battered.
Most of his injuries he overcame,
but his twisted nose is what got him his name.

He was called Broken Nose Scotty forevermore,
which seemed to add credence to his folklore.
It should be noted too, that he would do a good deed,
for anyone, anywhere who had more of a need.

Each week he worked his claim on Breece Hill,
then spent the weekends in the barrooms of Leadville,
where he loved to tell stories of his life in the sage,
and his harrowing experiences driving a stage.

One Saturday night Scotty became very disorderly and drunk,
and, consequently spent the night on a jailhouse bunk.
He had squandered his gold dust, and couldn't provide bail.
The jail was crowded, a perfect audience for a tale.

So, he told one story and then some more.
The inmates seemed to enjoy Scotty's lore,
and, in the process he made many new friends.
The good fortune that followed paid dividends.

To the jailhouse a well-dressed visitor came,
who offered to buy Scotty's Breece Hill claim.
His offer was magnanimous, one Scotty couldn't refuse.
The Lord has worked a miracle he thought, what great news.

Scotty was released, and they consummated the transmittal.
What a deal, he thought, for a claim that yielded so little.
In all the years of his life he had never seen so much dough.
It was like finding a pot of gold at the end of a rainbow.

He was ecstatic and wanted everyone to share his glee.
So, back to jail to pay some bail, and all his chums were set free.
They all went to the haberdashery, and were outfitted head to toe.
Then on to the most fashionable restaurant for steak and potato.

They ate and drank champagne, and then drank some more.
The more they drank, the more they swore.
Some fell from their chairs and couldn't get off the floor.
To the restaurateurs it was a situation to deplore.

"Disturbing the Peace" was the charge, and right back in jail.
After two days they let Scotty post bail.
He continued to spend his money as fast as he could.
Others helped him spend it, in the spirit of brotherhood.

He set up a trust to care for his mother who had a stroke,
and then spent the rest of his money until he was broke.
Broken Nose Scotty died a pauper, without pain and with ease,
with the county paying his burial fees.

A FRONTIER KITCHEN

Pioneers heading west had to rely
    on a wagon train cook,
for most of the grub
    of which they partook.

But once a family settled
    in a permanent place,
a cookery would be a housewife's
    first task to embrace.

To properly furnish her kitchen
    would be her mission.
A place where she could prepare meals
    that were high in nutrition.

Cooking over an open hearth,
    she would soon exchange,
with the major purchase of a
    wood burning range.

Her kitchen had to have
    a very large kettle,
constructed of heavy
    cast-iron metal.

Also, a nickel plated coffee pot,
    and a pie or cake pan,
as well as a spider
    or frying pan.

A spider is a cast-iron
    frying pan with short feet,
designed to stand among coals
    in the most intense heat.

Important were plates and cups
    made of enameled tin,
and without question she needed
    a rolling pin.

Iron spoons, knives and forks,
    for all of her clan,
and of value too was
    a water or milk can.

She certainly needed a
    revolving ice cream freezer.
Optional, and harder to come by were
    a butcher knife and lemon squeezer.

Some kitchens, settlers were
    able to modernize.
Those that couldn't
    simply had to improvise.

If a housewife had no baking pan
    for bacon or for bread,
she would cut green willow switches
    and simply use them instead.

By spearing slices of bacon, or rolls of dough
    with a sharpened willow spire,
and then cooking the goods by holding them
    over an open fire.

JUDGE ROY BEAN

In the days of the adventurous pioneer,
out on the plains of the western frontier,
there was one colorful character to behold,
of whom many tales and legends are told.

As railroad workers laid new tracks west,
Roy Bean and his tent saloon stayed abreast.
It was a place where the men could congregate,
get a little rowdy, and socially lubricate.

At Langtry, Texas they built a railroad station,
a settlement that Bean thought needed libation,
so, he built a permanent wood framed saloon,
complete with poker tables, a bar and spittoon.

You could even buy a bowl of chili,
at the place he named the Jersey Lilly.
He called himself Judge, 'cause there wasn't one close,
and claimed to be the "law west of the Pecos."

Texas Rangers with prisoners, he would accommodate,
'cause it was 200 miles to the nearest magistrate.
His saloon was his courtroom when trial time came,
and from there he gained his legendary fame.

Judge Roy Bean knew very little law,
so his proclamations were often received in awe.
Wedding ceremonies ended with his console,
"May God have mercy on your soul."

"You cannot grant divorces!" a federal judge once exhorted,
a demand to which Roy Bean promptly retorted,
"I married them, so I reckon I have the right,
to rectify my errors (and disunite)."

A worker fell, then bled, from a wound to his head,
until Roy Bean finally pronounced him dead.
The standard five dollar coroner's fee
was insufficient for his services, thought he.

On the dead man's body, he found 40 bucks and a gun.
With no complaint from the fellow whose life was done,
"I find this corpse guilty of carrying a concealed weapon,
so I fine it 40 dollars!" stated Bean with a grin.

When it came time for the murder trial of an Irishman,
who was convicted of killing a Chinese workman,
the courtroom was packed with an Irish crowd,
of rough-looking men who were boisterous and loud.

They were there to assure that the trial was fair,
and possibly threaten the judge with a scare.
As he leafed through his statutes, Bean surveyed the throng,
and realized this was a matter he shouldn't prolong.

"Although there are many prohibitions against homicide,"
stated Judge Bean, as he hastened to abide,
"there is no specific ban against killing a Chinese.
This case is dismissed."

Judge Roy Bean tried cases for nearly two decades,
and because of his truly unorthodox escapades,
(and unorthodox is the word to underscore,)
he etched his way into the annals of western lore.

CONTEMPLATING

A dictator threatened
   to assassinate my father.
Revenge is my primary goal,
   the dictator's death another.

What excuse could I give
   that the masses wouldn't deplore?
What excuse could I give
   for going to war?

And, if I started a conflict,
   would I one day be forgiven?
'Tis an uncertain end
   toward which I am driven.

A reason, a reason
   is what I need,
to initiate such
   a dastardly deed.

Behold, behold,
   I should have thought of this before,
it's the perfect excuse
   for starting a war.

I could lead the public
   in tragic misdirection,
by claiming the dictator
   has weapons of mass destruction.

CREEDE

If ever there was a red-hot boom town,
    the city of Creede was certainly it.
Following the discovery of very rich ore,
    t'was a melting pot of the fit and unfit.

Gunfighters mixed with miners and crooks,
    and once the railroad came,
speculators, gamblers and parlor girls
    arrived on every train.

Soapy Smith was a con-artist
    that no one wanted to cross.
He opened the Orleans Club and
    declared himself underworld boss.

For awhile, another saloon was run
    by the fairly reputable gun,
of the off-again, on-again lawman,
    the celebrated, Bat Masterson.

The Exchange, a dance hall and saloon,
    was owned by the coward Bob Ford,
the man who shot Jesse James in the back,
    in order to collect the reward.

A fellow named Ed O'Kelly
    entered the Exchange one day,
leveled his shotgun at Bob Ford,
    and blew the saloon owner away.

One of the slugs drove a collar button
    deep into Bob Ford's throat.
They buried his corpse at Boot Hill,
    alongside others who were smote.

At the request of his family, however,
    his body was later procured,.
Then sent to his Missouri hometown,
    where it was reinterred.

At Boot Hill, they didn't even have time
    to fill the empty grave with dirt.
For into the hole left by Bob Ford's carcass,
    another killer's corpse they did insert.

The parlor house "queens" were so ugly,
    it prompted the newspaper to say so,
"...some of her citizens would take
    sweepstake prizes at a hog show."

At one time or another,
    Creede had the distinction to claim,
three cigar-smoking female gamblers,
    Poker Alice, Killarney Kate, and Calamity Jane.

A fire in '92, and the silver crash of '93,
    were catalysts that caused Creede's doom,
resulting in a mass exodus from town,
    and spelled the end of the boom.

A GHOST TOWN

Visit an authentic ghost town,
    and appreciate the contrast,
as it is a really great way
    to step back into the past.

Flapping shutters and creaking boards
    will amplify your imagination,
and for the folks that once lived there,
    you'll have a greater appreciation.

Look down the main street and
    envision people at a busy pace,
with horses, burros, buggies,
    and buckboards commonplace.

Maybe it's Sunday and a lady is fit
    in a fur of muskrat,
while a gent sports a bow tie,
    white spats and top hat.

Could be it's the 4th of July,
    for here comes the parade,
with the hose team out front,
    from the fire brigade.

Well, however you choose
    to bring back the past,
you'll establish memories
    that will surely last.

But, let me offer a suggestion
    and I will guarantee,
that the closer you look,
    the more you will see.

Your images will be indelible
    and memories will prevail,
if you scrutinize and examine things
    in minute detail,

Check out the steps,
    for shoe and boot wear.
Are the heads on those battered nails
    round or square?

Were the door hinges hammered
    on an anvil with care,
or, did they come direct
    from a mail order hardware?

Some walls may be covered
    with a fancy wallpaper,
But, check the dates if they are
    pasted with newspaper.

Buildings constructed of square-hewn logs,
    though built with skill,
preceded those framed of boards,
    cut at a saw mill.

Some outhouses are flat, others have
    stairs to an elevated floor,
so a heavy snow can't
    block the door.

Visit an authentic ghost town,
    and appreciate the contrast,
as it is a really great way
    to step back into the past.

THE SALUTE

The Confederate troops marched northward,
    led by General Robert E Lee,
under the scorching hot sun,
    in June of 1863.

As they crossed the fields of Pennsylvania,
    heading toward Gettysburg,
a young girl ran from a nearby farmhouse,
    waving a Union flag.

She stood defiantly at the side of the road,
    as General Lee called his troops to a halt.
It was a bold and courageous thing,
    the general must have thought.

He studied the face of the girl,
    and then in a gesture quite resolute,
he raised his arm and ceremoniously
    gave her a firm salute.

When later asked why he saluted the enemy.
    Robert E. Lee observed,
"I saluted not the enemy, but the bravery of a young patriot,
    and the flag of a great nation that I once served."

PIROGUE ON THE BAYOU

Down on the Mississippi Delta
    where its water ways flow,
and the Gulf winds blow,
    and the land is low.

Louisianans call everything a bayou,
    whether it's a natural distributary,
or at river's end an estuary,
    or most any kind of tributary.

It matters not, whether it begins or ends
    in a river with no wake,
a marsh or swampy break,
    a huge or tiny lake,

The pirogue is a favorite cajun boat
    its design from a Choctaw dugout grew,
so similar in many ways to a canoe,
    and able to navigate the narrowest bayou.

The vessel is constructed by Acadians
    from a hollowed-out cypress log.
The hull and flat bottom of the pirogue
    allows it to be poled over a muddy bog.

Even in a dense swamp
    full of cypress knees and grassy weeds,
nothing seems to impede its speed,
    as the pirogue slides over marshy reeds.

One paddle easily propels the slender craft
    out on the open blue.
Cajuns even claim that the pirogue
    can glide on a heavy dew.

SIMPLE SAM

Simple Sam was an industrious man,
though obviously short on intellect.
He dreamed of owning a little land
on which a log cabin he could erect.

It had to be a lot he could afford,
for he had very little money to invest.
Finally, he found a place, he thought,
where he could build his little nest.

On the desert in Arizona,
was a cheaply priced tract of land.
It was so because for miles and miles,
all one could see was sand.

There was no water, nor were there trees,
but Sam thought the deal quite grand,
so he scraped together his money,
and purchased that sandy land.

In the midst of dunes of sand,
building his cabin was quite a feat.
He had a terrible time with footings,
just trying to pour concrete.

To build where there were no trees,
was a decision without foresight,
and the logs he purchased in the city,
was a choice that wasn't too bright.

It didn't matter that the structure was flimsy,
or that Simple Sam was down on his luck,
'cause the cabin wasn't finished one week,
before terrible tragedy struck.

It seems that maybe he worked too hard,
and fell asleep with a lit cigar,
for the cabin and Sam went up in smoke,
in a blaze that could've been seen afar.

There might be a moral to this story,
a lesson to be learned if you're smart.
If you plan to construct a cabin,
don't use fireplace logs from Wal-Mart.

GAY RIGHTS AND WRONGS

Some states allow a woman
    to wed another woman,
and likewise a man
    to marry a man.

But different strokes
    for different folks,
will quite often
    a fire stoke.

We shouldn't judge, nor say
    that a gay can't live with a gay.
But to a marriage of a duo that's gay,
    we should all say nay.

Adoption of children by gays,
    is a more important subject to raise.
There are certain values of gays,
    that a child shouldn't have to appraise.

Gay rights we should pursue,
    but, bid the wrongs adieu.
Gay adoption of children
    should be strictly taboo.

PEGLEG BODEEN

I must tell you the story of Pegleg Bodeen,
the bravest man that Alaska has ever seen.
North of the Arctic Circle he carried the mail,
where furry creatures and Eskimos prevail.

He would deliver to each igloo and household,
in a place where the weather is so very cold,
that the leather would freeze on his dog sled reins.
as he traveled across the Arctic Plains.

He wore his hair long, with a raggedy looking beard,
So no one could see that he was lop-eared.
He was a large man with muscles that rippled,
but he gained his fame when he became crippled.

When his dogs were attacked by a Kodiak bear,
he leaped to their rescue, without despair.
It was much like the David and Goliath tale,
He had only a knife, cut from the bone of a whale.

It was his only protection from that huge Kodiak,
but Bodeen was brave and wouldn't fall back.
He thrust his knife forward, and punctured one eye,
as the bear tore Bodeen's leg off at the thigh.

From one leg, Bodeen lunged through the air
and stabbed with aplomb the other eye of the bear.
The raging, blind Kodiak whirled and ran,
defeated by the brave Arctic Plains mailman.

Pegleg Bodeen lost his leg, and the bear his sight,
in Alaska's most famous bear and man fight.
Now, there isn't much humor to find in the after show,
until you visualize a pegleg mailman walking on snow.

Above the Arctic Circle the snow doesn't quit,
and to walk on a pegleg is like walking on a drill bit.
Bodeen later solved the problem, I should mention,
by retiring to Florida with a government pension.

WHISKEY LAKE

Between Window Rock and Shiprock,
in the historic Navajo Nation block,
there is a remote and tranquil location,
at a high-altitude destination.

Amidst juniper and aspen trees,
where leaves flutter in the cool breeze,
is an ideal spot to take a break,
at the serenity of Whiskey Lake.

It's a perfect place for a getaway,
on a hot and muggy summer day.
For those who have their bait and pole,
it's also a fantastic fishing hole,

An angler will never ever strike out,
for the lake is well-stocked with trout.
Rainbow or cutthroat, catch-as-catch-can,
out of the lake and into a frying pan.

Chuska Mountains with many a treetop,
provide a lovely, breathtaking backdrop,
to the shoreline of Whiskey Lake,
an ideal spot to take a break.

HOW POLITICIANS DUCK QUESTIONS

'Tis the art of dodging,
evading and hedging,
that enables digression
when answering a question.

Politicians have mastered the skill
and respond by sidestepping at will.
They may reply by asking another question,
or answer with a vague generalization.

A reaction that shows neglect,
is to simply change the subject.
Or, comment on the subject enthusiastically,
without answering the question specifically.

A common response to an inquiry of why,
is that someone else is better qualified to reply.
Or, by stating that the question is irrelevant,
to honor one with an answer, they shan't.

A politician might stand behind the protection,
that the answer is classified or privileged information.
Whatever the dodge, and there are many,
is there a politician anywhere, that doesn't use any?

MY '55 T-BIRD

The Thunderbird, introduced in '55 by Ford,
was a sports compact that America could afford.

In a world of the overstyled and overchromed car,
its clean and subtle lines certainly raised the bar.

In dealer showrooms, by comparison,
it outsold the Corvette 24 to 1.

The T-Bird boasted a Mercury V-8,
that salespeople loved to demonstrate.

What a great car, I thought, and purchased one,
a rayon-top convertible that was second to none.

I really loved my '55,
with stick-shift and overdrive.

The engine had an output of 200 horsepower,
and a top speed of 114 miles per hour.

The hood scoop covered a four-barrel carb,
and the interior was fashioned in graceful garb.

The dashboard sported a high-mounted speedometer,
and to gauge revolutions it had a tachometer.

Of style and prestige, it was a marvelous blend,
and it had reliability on which I could depend.

My Thunderbird two-seater of '55,
was simply an awesome pleasure to drive.

Today, the stylish car is an icon of design.
I certainly wish that I still had mine.

COCKEYED GAIL

Gail is a beautiful female,
    except for one small detail.
When one of her eyes is looking at you
    the other seems to derail.

She can attract most any male
    as long as she wears her veil.
But when she exposes her cocked eye,
    men swiftly turn tail.

With her good eye, Gail
    can read books and her mail.
If she closes it, however,
    she'd have to use braille.

A fantastic cook is Gail,
    who can serve up a sumptuous regale.
But if one were to view her cocked eye,
    a taxi they would promptly hail..

An invite for a dinner of baked quail,
    would be a treat for any male.
And, she is always the life of a party,
    as long as she doesn't unveil.

Like the song of a nightingale,
    is the tender, sweet voice of Gail.
But when she exposes her cocked eye,
    men hastily hit the trail.

To take her out for a cocktail,
    would be a pleasure for any male.
But when out on a date, if she were to unveil,
    the date he would promptly curtail.

From one to ten on a scale,
    she's a ten if she wears her veil.
But when she exposes her cocked eye,
    men always set sail.

She's healthy, hearty and hale,
    not weak, frail and pale.
But, to kiss her is another thing,
    for to do so she'd have to unveil.

Affairs would rapidly go stale.
    Was there any chance one might not fail?
The prospect of marriage was nil, she thought,
    so she would often sit home and wail.

A relationship would certainly prevail,
    however, for Cockeyed Gail.
And, one could wager the chances are good that
    it would never fail.

If she simply told an ideal male,
    that on the day she wears her wedding veil,
of her huge net worth he could avail,
    for she is heir to the empire of Bloomingdale.

THE PORTLAND HEAD LIGHT

From Cape Elizabeth,
    a light shines bright,
from the lens atop
    the Portland Head Light.

It's visible from afar
    to a navigator's sight,
for approaching vessels,
    all through the night.

When the federal government
    came into being, in 1789,
it assumed responsibility for
    aids to navigation, in act number 9.

To the Treasury Department,
    this duty, it consigned,
and completion of the Portland Head
    the bill further defined.

Construction had been initiated by Massachusetts,
    in the area later to become Maine,
and by late 1790 under the auspices of the U.S.
    completion it would attain.

The lighthouse officially opened,
    with its first keeper, Joseph Greenleaf,
as sixteen lamps filled with whale oil
    cast a beam from the rocky reef.

In 1886, during the shipwreck
    of the *Anna C. Maguire,*
an act of heroism occurred,
    that we should all admire.

Keeper Joshua Strout and his son Joseph
    in a most remarkable deed,
saved the lives of the captain and crew
    by acting with courage and speed.

For more than three generations the Strouts
    served as keepers at the site,
of America's most photographed lighthouse,
    the Portland Head Light.

FAT RAT AND HEARTLESS MATT

Fat Rat was a vengeful rat
    who made his home in the 3-story house
that was owned by heartless Matt,
    and Dove his ugly, overbearing spouse.

Their marriage was usually tit for tat,
    and for years there hadn't been love.
In one ear, and out the other of Matt,
    went the unreasonable demands of Dove.

She would daily call him a pitiful louse,
    and everything he did she'd detest.
Matt was continually in her doghouse,
    but he really was a pest.

Now speaking of pests, we must discuss Fat Rat,
    the rodent who dwelled in their home.
The large house was a great place to make his habitat,
    for he needed a lot of space to roam.

And in that expanse there was much he could destroy,
    for he could gnaw as well as any polecat.
Nor could he find more obnoxious people to annoy,
    then ugly Dove and heartless Matt.

Matt had a Stetson hat that he nearly always wore,
    except when he slept or bathed.
That broad-brimmed felt hat, he really did adore,
    and even wore it when he shaved.

One day heartless Matt was so incensed
    after Fat Rat had devoured all their bread,
that he set rat traps all over the residence,
    and swore the rat soon would be dead.

After several close calls, Fat Rat retaliated,
    by chewing the Stetson to bits.

The hat was shredded, and Matt was infuriated.
    Dove laughed at his anger fits.

Down to the haberdashery he went
    to buy a new broad-brimmed hat.
He certainly resented all of the torment
    being caused by Dove and Fat Rat.

The next day while outside burning some trash
    he spotted Fat Rat in the yard.
Matt gave chase with a furious dash.
    He may never have run so hard.

He caught that rodent and without thinking twice
    threw Fat Rat into the fire.
To burn alive, thought Matt, is to pay the price,
    certain that the rat would expire.

The rodent, however, unbeknownst to Matt,
    sprinted from the flames afire.
Back into the house scampered Fat Rat,
    and he ran about spreading the fire.

When he noticed smoke pouring from the house,
    Matt dashed through the open door.
He spotted the woman that always called him a louse.
    Dove was lying on the kitchen floor.

He raced through the house, from room to room,
    searching for his broad-brimmed hat.
'Til the roof collapsed, spelling poor Matt's doom,
    as well as Dove and Fat Rat.

When authorities discovered Matt's remains
    there were traces of a hat on his head.
Oh well, they might all be better off,
    but that should probably go unsaid.

BILTMORE HOUSE

Ashville, North Carolina, boasts
    a most extraordinary place,
an incredible 250-room mansion
    with four acres of floor space.

George Vanderbilt III
    had a dream to create
a magnificent chateau
    as his country estate.

One thousand artisans
    slaved for six long years,
before they could hang
    the last chandeliers.

There were local laborers
    making 50 cents per day,
and acclaimed sculptors
    at a high rate of pay.

Because Vanderbilt was such
    a masterful planner,
the Biltmore House and Gardens
    rivals any European manor.

Upon completion in 1895,
    there was a total of 34 bedrooms,
65 fireplaces, 3 kitchens,
    and no less than 43 bathrooms.

Fine landscape and architecture
    highlight the grand exterior.
Priceless furnishings and art
    adorn the posh interior.

Among its multitude of amenities,
    it was equipped with elevators,
and a rarity for the nineteenth century,
    it even had refrigerators.

The Vanderbilts were attended
    by an 80-person staff,
that worked very long hours
    on their master's behalf.

With 23,000 volumes of books
    in Vanderbilt's collection,
the staff included a librarian
    who cataloged for selection.

The huge Banquet Hall, a room
    spirited with medieval feeling,
is 72 feet long, 42 feet wide, with
    a 70 foot high vaulted ceiling.

It was designed to display unique
    hanging tapestries,
that tell the love affair of Venus and Mars
    in a 5-part series.

The dining table can accommodate
    up to 64 for a party of choice,
and with perfect acoustics surrounding
    one need not raise their voice.

A score in the billiard room
    one could tally,
or compete on the two-lane
    bowling alley.

When the Carolina sun was hot,
    one could opt for cool,
by taking a dip in the
    indoor swimming pool.

The 3-mile approach road
    before you arrive,
has ponds, streams and flowers,
    a beautiful drive.

The Biltmore House is
    a most extraordinary place,
an incredible 250-room mansion,
    with four acres of floor space.

PIG WRESTLING

While visiting in Suskanoo,
I said, "There's nothing here to do."
My friend pulled out a chaw to chew,
and said, "We have a thing or two.
There is a sunset for you to view,
or pig wrestling to entertain you."

He wiped the sweat from his underarm,
"My cousin's a babe with lots of charm,
her fee is ten bucks, no cause for alarm,
she wrestles a pig but induces no harm."
I said, "No," but he twisted my arm,
then drove me to his uncle's farm.

His bikini-clad cousin was no dud.
He said, "Here's ten bucks from my bud."
The pig in his pen was chewing his cud.
She turned on the hose, the sty to flood,
to make a slushy, mushy bog of mud,
then pushed the pig into all that crud.

Then into the mud bog she did climb.
She rolled around with the swine for a time,
until they both were covered with slime,
after a while the slime turned to grime.
This wasn't worth a look or a stime,
It seemed like such a pitiful crime.

That poor pig seemed ready to cry,
if he hadn't had so much mud in each eye.
To watch a human with a pig vie,
was so vile and gross, I later asked why.
The event could be loved by any horsefly,
but I was ready to leave that foul sty.

Before leaving Suskanoo,
I said, "There's nothing here to do."
My friend pulled out a chaw to chew,
and said, "We have a thing or two.
There is a sunset for you to view,
or you can go watch the cows moo."

SARCASTIC CAMPER

Dark skies are severed by flashes of light,
as rain pelts our tent all through the night.
Thunder rolls, and twisters may form.
It's a joy to camp out in a wicked storm.

Soggy logs will burn when they are split,
'cause they're dry inside and can be lit.
But, to build a fire in a driving rain,
is quite futile, for you will toil in vain.

So, for supper we had a most tasty treat,
of cold beans and bread without any meat.
Breakfast should also be quite a smash,
more bread with cold corned beef hash.

Like the rhythm of music in weather so foul,
the tent will sway and the wind will howl.
Thunder rolls, and twisters may form.
It's a joy to camp out in a wicked storm.

PLACES WITH GOOFY NAMES

There are many places with unusual names
across our vast and beautiful land.
How some of these spots got their names
is certainly difficult to understand.

From the community of *Rifle* to *Gun Barrel Road*,
or towns like *Rodeo*, *Roundup* and *Spur*,
to *Cut and Shoot*, where many a cowboy rode,
are places you will find out west for sure.

In New Mexico's *Truth or Consequences*,
or, Louisiana's town of *Plain Dealing*,
justice seems to be the rule,
and you might get shot for cheating.

There's *Ham Lake*, *Hog Park Reservoir*,
and, who would want to swim in *Sour Lake*.
Or, *Sleepy Eye* and *Sleepy Hollow*
to the old mining camp called *Wide Awake*.

Illinois has a place named *Oblong*,
although that isn't the shape of the city.
Washington has a village called *Concrete*.
Those that live there you'd have to pity.

Texas has many a water source,
from *Coldspring* to *Dripping Springs*.
Billy the Kid was once caught in New Mexico,
at a place called *Stinking Springs*.

You'll find *Sinking Spring* in Pennsylvania.
Other springs certainly sound aglow,
like the *Red Boiling Springs* in Tennessee,
or the *Lava Hot Springs in Idaho*.

Speaking of hot, it's important to mention,
that Hawaii has a village called *Volcano*.
Who would want to live in such a place,
T'would be as bad as West Virginia's *Tornado*.

In the densely populated state of New Jersey,
there is a place called *Ho-ho-kus*.
Is that what a magician says?
Or is it hokus pokus?

In *Deaf Smith County*, Texans prepare their chaw,
'cause on a good supply of Skoal they must rely.
Illinois and West Virginia each have a *Paw Paw*.
Near *Enigma*, Georgia is the town of *Ty Ty*.

West Virginia also has a *Crab Orchard*,
and *Junior* is the only place so named in all the land.
Its neighbor Virginia has a *Burnt Chimney*,
and towns called *Horse Pasture* and *Goochland*.

While there are lots of farms across this land,
Arizona has a burg called *Many Farms*.
Kentucky has a *Dwarf*, and also *Broad Fields*,
so it likewise has room for many farms.

There's a hamlet in Kentucky known as *Horse Cave*,
and in Tennessee a *Hollow Rock*.
In North Carolina there is a spot called *Bat Cave*,
near the attraction, *Chimney Rock*.

The mat is out in *Welcome*, Louisiana,
but obviously not in *Cut Off*, further down the road.
The welcome mat is also out in *Bar Nunn, Wyoming*,
and maybe so in *Ten Sleep*, which must have one abode.

Wyoming also has a town named *Smoot*,
What on earth is a smoot? Do you wonder?
That lightening is scary is a point quite mute,
but be it known that Minnesota has *Good Thunder*.

Michigan has two towns that should get together.
Bad Axe is not far from *Grind Stone City*.
Tho' there's no commode, there is a *Flushing*.
You'd think that place would be a little gritty

Thousands of kids mail their requests
to *Santa Claus*, Indiana, each year.
With the hope that Dancer and Prancer,
don't wind up like Montana's *Lame Deer*.

Sometimes these unusual places,
are in close proximity to each other.
It makes one wonder if there's a connection,
from the naming of one to another.

For instance, in Brown County, Indiana,
near Nashville, with its artists galore,
are the communities of *Beanblossom*,
Stone Head, *Gnaw Bone* and *Needmore*.

On the North Carolina coast, near Kitty Hawk,
site of the Wright Brothers milestone,
are the villages of *Duck*, *Kill Devil Hills*,
Nags Head, *Spot* and *Whalebone*.

To the south is the picturesque island of *Ocracoke*.
where Pepsi is the preferred drink.
It's near the site where Blackbeard did croak,
and where many ships were known to sink.

Missouri has *Black Jack* and *Knob Noster*,
and Colorado its *Dinosaur*.
We could probably go on with this foolishness,
but for now there is no more.

OTHER WORKS BY DAVE SOUTHWORTH

BOOKS: NONFICTION

Famous Gunfights of the American West
Famous Gunfights of Texas
Gunfighters of the Old West
Gunfighters of the Old West II
Feuds on the Western Frontier
Leadville
Colorado Gold Dust: Short Stories and Profiles
Ghost Towns and Mining Camps of the San Juans
Colorado Mining Camps

BOOKS: FICTION

Franklin Hall

VIDEOS

Colorado Mining Camps: A Pictorial Treasure of the Gold and Silver Boom
Leadville: The Boom Years
Mining Camps of the San Juans
Cripple Creek and the Mining Camps of Teller County
The Mining Camps of Northwest Colorado
Boulder County Mining Camps: A Look Back
The Mining Camps of Gilpin and Clear Creek Counties
The Mining Camps of South Central Colorado

AUDIO BOOKS

Colorado Gold Dust: Short Stories and Profiles
Gunfighters of the Old West
Billy the Kid and the Lincoln County War
Jesse James and the James-Younger Gang
Doc Holliday and the Earp Brothers